The Approaching Winter

The Approaching Winter

The Next Great Depression

Don Braby

authorHOUSE™

1663 LIBERTY DRIVE, SUITE 200
BLOOMINGTON, INDIANA 47403
(800) 839-8640
WWW.AUTHORHOUSE.COM

First published by AuthorHouse 11/29/05

ISBN: 1-4208-8059-4 (sc)

Library of Congress Control Number: 2005907668

Printed in the United States of America
Bloomington, Indiana

This book is printed on acid-free paper.

Table of Contents

Acknowledgments

It's amazing what it takes to write a book. I have a great admiration for all authors that undertake such a task. I also appreciate all those that spend countless hours of editing and critiquing manuscripts. Special thanks to my editor, Kurt Florman at <u>www.proof-it.com</u> for his work. Also, this book would not have been written without the help of my friends Dave Downey, who is an accomplished writer in his own right, Mary Scollard and Truly Griffin for their expertise. Thanks also to Cliff Collar for the cover photo.

Foreword

The Approaching Winter: The Next Great Depression is a book that combines U.S. history and America's ever repeating cycles with a psychology that has been slowly changing form since the turn of the century. Within the next few years, America will have to come to grips with an approaching economic winter that could result in the worst depression in its 230 years of history. What we thought our children's children would have to struggle through may be ours to endure.

As this book was being published by Author House, Americans experienced yet another great tragedy upon our soul as Hurricane Katrina ripped through the Gulf of Mexico coastline. This catastrophe, 9/11 and perhaps future events may be the triggers that will usher in the next great depression.

As you read *The Approaching Winter: The Next Great Depression*, it may cause you to be fearful, angry and uncertain of our future. However, by reading this book you may be able to prepare yourself psychologically and perhaps economically to face the stormy and bitterly cold winter that awaits each and every one of us.

"The reasonable man
adapts himself to the world.
The unreasonable man persists
in trying to adapt the world to himself.
Therefore, all progress depends on the
unreasonable man."

George Bernard Shaw
1935 Nobel prize winner
1856-1950

Chapter 1

History, Cycles, And The Stock Market

As Americans, we truly are a blessed people. We have everything we want. We have the best jobs in the world. We have the best cars. We have the best homes. Ours is the highest standard of living enjoyed since the creation of the world. In the roaring 90s, we witnessed the longest economic expansion in the history of the United States as well as a bull market unequaled since this country was founded. Life has been grand. Talk of a New Era or a New Economy was widespread late in the decade. Financial prophets proclaimed prosperity for everyone. In 2003 and 2004 both the stock market and the economy recovered from the mini recession of 2001 and established a positive upward trend.

But the question we must ask ourselves is, will this trend continue beyond 2005? Better yet, can it? Can the United States continue an endless ascension into greater and greater prosperity? Or are we destined to repeat the same patterns and cycles of history? And can we catch a glimpse of our future if we cast but a glance at our past?

United States History Points to our Future

Our country's history shows, very clearly, that after every major economic expansion a major correction always follows. In the Roaring Twenties, an enormous stock market rise and economic boom gave way to the Great Depression. The middle of the 19th century also saw an expansion followed by a depression.

In fact, if we examine the totality of our history, dating all the way back to Independence, we find that a cycle repeats itself on the average every 75 years. Every 75 years or so, the United States plunges into a crisis that lasts several years and sometimes as long as 20 years. The first such crisis was the American Revolutionary War in 1780. The second was the Civil War in 1860. And the third was the Great Depression, which began in 1930. Are we about to enter a fourth era of extreme hardship?

Before answering that question, perhaps we ought to tackle this one: Does history really repeat itself? In our quest for the answer, let us consider the following, very telling quotes about the America of the 1920s.

1. *"There will be no interruption of our permanent prosperity."* Myron E. Forbes, President, Pierce Arrow Motor Car Co., January 12, 1928.[1]

2. *"No Congress of the United States ever assembled, on surveying the state of the Union,*

has met with a more pleasing prospect than that which appears at the present time...and the highest record of years of prosperity." Calvin Coolidge, December 4, 1928.[2]

3. *"In most of the cities and towns of this country, this Wall Street panic will have no effect."* Paul Block, President of the Block newspaper chain, editorial, November 15, 1929.[3]

4. "*Stocks have reached what looks like a permanently high plateau.*" Irving Fisher, Professor of Economics, Yale University, 1929.[4]

Now let's fast-forward to 1966 and examine the words of Alan Greenspan, one of the foremost financial officials of our time. This is what he said was the cause of the Great Depression:

"The excess credit which the Fed pumped into the economy spilled over into the stock market — triggering a fantastic speculative boom. Belatedly, Federal Reserve officials attempted to sop up the excess reserves and finally succeeded in braking the boom. But it was too late: by 1929 the speculative imbalances had become so overwhelming that the attempt precipitated a sharp retrenching and a constant demoralizing of business confidence. As a result the American economy collapsed." [5]

Sounds a lot like our day, doesn't it? Today, observers could just as easily suggest the Fed has pumped so much credit into the economy that it has spilled into the housing market and triggered another speculative boom. It's hard to believe, that after promoting several years of "easy money" or "easy credit," the powerful Federal Reserve chairman doesn't seem to remember what he said back in 1966.

Will today's excess credit trigger the same phenomenon history recorded of the 1920s and 1930s? It has often been said that if you don't learn from your mistakes you will repeat them over and over.

The Roaring Twenties

The Roaring Twenties was famous for its excessive indulgence, something that has come to define the 1990s and today as well. Compare the events of those very different, yet very similar periods and it becomes unmistakably clear: History is beginning to repeat. As we continue to explore this very disturbing reality, let's take a look at some of the key events of those Roaring Twenties.

June 5, 1920: Passage of the oil and coal land-leasing act lays the foundation for the biggest Washington scandal of the decade.

March 6, 1922: Babe Ruth signs a three-year contract with baseball's New York Yankees for a salary of $52,000 a year, the highest salary for a ballplayer up to then.

March 25, 1922: Women's fashions, with hemlines to the knee and beyond, are deemed so revealing that Catholic Pope Pius XI urges a campaign against them.

<u>May 10, 1924</u>: J. Edgar Hoover is appointed director of the scandal-plagued Bureau of Investigation (later renamed the FBI) with the charge of restoring the agency integrity and effectiveness.

<u>Sept 10, 1924</u>: The trial of the decade: Nathan Leopold, 19, and Richard Loeb,18, who kidnaped and murdered a 14-year-old boy on May 22 for sport, are sentenced to life in prison. The case was noted for the murderers' cold lack of remorse and because that they had come from a privileged background and had excelled in academics.

<u>Nov. 7, 1924</u>: A stock market boom that began early in the decade hits a five-year high with 2.33 million shares traded on the New York Stock Exchange.

<u>Dec 7, 1927</u>: U.S. Senate refuses to seat Senator-elect Frank Smith from Illinois because the $485,000 he spent on his campaign was deemed unethically high. Two days later the same thing happens to Senator-elect William Vare of Pennsylvania.[6]

Simply put, history repeats itself because people repeat history. America is about to repeat a very dark part of its history because those that lead our country are making the same type of mistakes that leaders made in the Twenties. It is inevitable. America is about to enter a crisis that may turn out to be the deepest depression in our history. Why will it be the deepest? Because we have so far to fall. Remember, it is we who are enjoying the highest standard of living the world has ever seen.

Things that will destroy America

Furthermore, it is interesting to note that in the early 1900s former President Theodore Roosevelt suggested, "The things that will destroy America are prosperity at any price, peace at any price, safety first instead of duty first, the love of soft living, and the get rich quick theory of life."[7] As a nation we are fulfilling Roosevelt's prophecy. The government is determined to make the current level of prosperity as permanent as possible, no matter what the cost. That is at least partly why our leaders are spending billions of dollars to keep the peace around the world. (Of course, some would say we've spent billions making new enemies and poking our noses into other people's business.) Also, we Americans are driven on finding ways to increase our already high standard of living and retire with a sizeable nest egg. Of course, who wouldn't want that? The problem is, as Roosevelt foresaw, "the love of soft living and the get rich quick theory of life" is not healthy for the nation. It tends to create an even more lopsided imbalance between rich and poor. If America continues down this road, she may be a third world country with no middle class in less than a decade.

Cycles That go Around and Around

Life is a cycle. We are born. At age five or six we start attending school. Most of us go on to graduate from high school. Some attend college, while others marry and raise a family. We work most of our lives, hoping to retire in comfort. And yes, then we die. The cycle of life is something we accept and understand just as we do the seasons of the year. I will never forget those widely varying seasons I experienced growing up in Iowa. We had bitterly cold winters, rainy and stormy springs, hot and muggy summers, and beautiful, cool autumns. The cycles of climate and life are very understandable and easy to predict. Not so, business and economic cycles. Those are tough even for the experts to get their hands around. Economists tend to be wrong more than they are right.

A key to understanding economics is the business cycle, a period of economic expansion followed by economic contraction. For the most part, the peak of each expansion occurred every three to five years from World War II through 1982. However, the period from 1983 to 2000 was marked by one of the two longest expansions in our history. Only from 1990–1991 did the economy contract during that remarkable 18-year run. And since 2000, President Bush has managed to avoid a major recession and to win re-election in November 2004 by lowering the overnight interest rates and by slashing taxes.

On the surface, it may sound like Bush is a genius when it comes to mastering the economy. But there is a problem. The 2001 minor recession did not fully correct the imbalances that have only grown larger as a result of Bush's financial policy.

The bottom line is that the contractions of the last 20 years have been nowhere near normal. Expansions are being forced to last longer and contractions are being artificially shortened by the Federal Reserve's actions, such as its manipulation of the overnight interest rate. When the Fed controls the rate instead of letting it flow naturally as in a free market, bigger bubbles develop and those trigger bigger crashes. The Federal Reserve is creating sort of a perfect storm because it has been reacting to economic conditions instead of allowing for the proper flow of the normal business cycle. Most economists break down economic cycles in months, years, or decades. However, a book written by William Strauss and Neil Howe called *The Fourth Turning* shows us a different type of cycle. They write about a cycle that has four seasons like our climate called turnings.

"The **First Turning** is a High (spring), an upbeat of strengthening institutions and weakening individualism, when a new civic order implants and the old value regime decays.

"The **Second Turning** is an Awakening (summer), a passionate era of spiritual upheaval, when the civic order comes under attack from a new value regime.

"The **Third Turning** is an Unraveling (fall), a downcast era of strengthening individualism and weakening institutions, when the old civic order decays and the new value regime implants.

"The **Fourth Turning** is a Crisis (winter), a decisive era of secular upheaval, when the value regime propels the replacement of the old civic order with a new one."[8]

According to the authors each of these turnings lasts about 20 years — the same length of time as a generation. One cycle of four turnings roughly matches the span of a human life. If you live to be 80 or 85 chances are you will have lived through a complete cycle. As well, each season or turning blends into the next, as our climatic seasons do. As we make the transition from spring to summer, there are weeks of cool days mixed with warm ones. Temperatures do not soar from 40 degrees to 90 degrees in one day and stay there. Similarly, there is a transition period between one turning and the next. The time it takes to entirely travel from one turning to the next is usually between three to five years.

The authors also say there are four different types of generations, which determine what type of turning will occur at a particular time. According to Strauss and Howe, "at the start of each turning, people change how they feel about themselves, the culture, the nation, and the future. Each turning comes with its own identifiable mood. These mood shifts can catch people by surprise."[9]

As each generation comes and goes, so comes a new turning. In recent history, the first turning, which was a time of celebration, reigned from 1946 to 1964. Our boys were coming home after a hard fought victory in World War II. The industrial age was alive and well. Optimism was soaring throughout the nation. Even the sky was not the limit. In the early 1960s, President John F. Kennedy proclaimed that we would reach the moon by the decade's end, which, of course, would turn out to be true. But all that optimism came to a screeching halt with his assassination. His death ushered in the second turning, which Strauss and Howe call "The Awakening"—a twenty-year period from 1964 to 1984.

A new mood of negativity, rebellion, and hatred descended like a dark cloud over the United States. From the Vietnam War to the hippie movement to the Beatles on the Ed Sullivan Show, signs were abundant that a new turning had arrived. This one would spawn the feminist, environmental, and other political movements that would play major roles in shaping our society. The turning also triggered sharp increases in crime and divorce rates, and it happened to occur during the last major bear market.

Then came the third turning. We accepted the changes that took place in the second turning and moved on. In 1984, the shift to a new season was perhaps illustrated best by Apple Computer's Super Bowl commercial showing a young lady sledge-hammering 1950s stone-faced men on a large video screen. This was a knockout blow to Big Blue —the IBM mainframe —and the birth of the personal computer age.

Also born at that time was the individualism era, which Strauss and Howe call the "Unraveling." By the mid-1990s it had become clear that the cornerstone of American society— the family— was deteriorating. "In 1984, Americans were first noticing that the conventional family was no longer the norm and premarital teen sex no longer a rarity. A decade later, married couples with children had shrunk to only 26 percent of all households (versus 40 percent in 1970), and the share of sexually active fifteen-year-old girls had swollen to 26 percent (versus 5 percent in 1970)."[10]

Any time now, the pace of the unraveling will increase as we enter twenty years of winter—the next major, long-lasting crisis. Most people will not know what hit them. They will be totally caught off guard. But there are signs out there.

The Bear Market and The True Bottom

As of this writing, the Dow Jones index has been struggling to make any upward movement since January 2004. What investors thought would be a new bull market will turn out to be one of the longest bear market rallies in our history. The Dow Jones and other markets are slowing rolling over as investors begin to fret about rising interest rates and the potential for runaway inflation.

The markets are rolling over much like a cresting ocean wave. During the growing momentum of a wave, there comes a time when water can rise no higher. As forces decrease and no longer are effective against the always-present and formidable pressure of gravity, the crest arrives and the wave crashes down. As for the waves rolling through the financial ocean, the Dow Jones and other markets have already passed their crests. Greed and the desire to buy more stocks fueled the bear market rally since 2003, but fear and panic will trigger a major sell-off and possibly a crash some time in 2006 or 2007.

As market prices fall, the investing world will be rocked by another wave of business scandals. In the business world when production numbers begin to decrease, business men and women tend to let their emotions take over. To satisfy stock holders, business leaders make irrational, foolish decisions that eventually force them to "cook" their books. Obviously, when stock prices rise, "Don't rock the boat," is the theme song around the company's staff meeting. The whistle-blower is never welcomed. But when stocks plummet, tough questions are asked about the balance sheet and income statement. Soon new companies will rise up to take the unenviable place of Enron, MCI World Com, Tyco, and Arthur Andersen.

Ok you might be saying, but what about the economy? Admittedly, in the early part of 2005, it looked pretty good. But rising interest rates will stop it cold. Furthermore, the economy does not lead the stock markets. It follows the markets' lead. As the stock market indices continue their downward trend, the economy won't be far behind.

You might be thinking, what about corporate profits? No doubt corporate profits have been rising steadily for the several quarters running. But don't forget profits were increasing in 1987 too. Then came the October 1987 crash. In that month, the Dow Jones plunged from 2,648 to 1,745—a free-fall of 34 percent, or roughly one-third of the value of the stock market. Today, as in 1987, exceptions are extremely high. Most investors believe corporate profits will continue to increase.

Furthermore, several investors say they believe the markets bottomed out in October 2002 and that a new bull market as begun. However, history tells us that lasting market bottoms tend to occur when the economy is still slipping, not when it's peaking. It was in August 1982 that the Dow Jones hit its last major bottom. On August 15 of that year, a *New York Times* article by William G. Shepherd Jr. titled "Dark Days on Wall Street" suggested that the bear market of the early 1980s still had one more leg to go. "In the past two weeks," Shepherd wrote, "all the market averages have plunged to new lows as Wall Street, beset by cruel economic news from all sides, has time after time been unable to mount a sustained rally. That is a discouraging omen, an indication that the bottom has not been reached and a sign that even the most steel willed optimists may be about to throw in their towels." Shepherd went on, "The economic upturn is nowhere in sight. It did not appear in the second quarter of the year, as many people had hoped. It does not seem to be appearing in the third quarter either. Corporate profits are continuing to slide."[11]

Historically, major market lows occur when there are more bears than bulls and when price/earnings ratios are between 5 and 8. However, according to Market Vane's Bullish Consensus, 69 percent of investors were bullish during a 3-week period in June 2005. "The percentage of bulls has now outnumbered the bears every week since the Dow's bottom in October 2002, 140 straight."[12] Furthermore, most stock's P/E ratios in the Dow Jones and the NASDAQ are currently 20 or higher.

Major market bottoms also tend to hit when no one is looking. According to Shepherd, several investors predicted the bottom in the Dow would strike somewhere between 550 and 650. Most thought for sure it would come at some number below 700. Like today's investor who is counting on the markets to continue their upward climb, the 1982 investor thought the bottom would never materialize. It did, however, on August 9, when the market hit 769.97. And guess what? No one was looking. It struck, in fact, six days before Mr. Shepherd's article was published, when "the economic upturn (was) nowhere in sight."

Investors, homeowners, business men and women and politicians do not see the storm, the perfect storm, that is about to engulf them. For them it's business as usual. But that does not change the fact that bloated government and consumer debt, business scandals, overvalued stocks, and the general lack of strong political leadership are the primary elements that will trigger the perfect economic storm: A crash of the stock markets and the deepest depression in the history of the United States. We are about to repeat history once again.

Chapter 2

The American Psyche

On September 10, 2001, the last thing on Americans' minds was the potential for an attack to be launched on our soil from another country. That all changed, of course, the morning of Sept. 11, when a pair of jumbo jets smashed through the glassy, metallic skin of the twin towers of the World Trade Center in New York City and a third jet drilled into the Pentagon near the nation's Capitol. And shall we never forget the fourth jet that crashed in Pennsylvania after several heroic Americans tried to take over the plane.

At that time, we rallied around our president as one. We took our flags out of our closets to show the world we stood behind our country. We prayed by candlelight for strength and for the comfort of those who had lost family and friends. For a while, this country was shaken to the point it actually turned to God. But what has happened since that unforgettable day? What happened to that spirit of unity and of helping one another that was so widespread in the days and weeks after the tragedy?

What Has Happened to Our Thinking?

Sadly, many of us now are going on with life as if 9/11 never happened. We are beginning to forget the unforgettable. While those in New York and Washington live with daily reminders, for many of us the attack is a distant memory. That is especially true of those who live from the Midwest to the West Coast.

True, perhaps all of us will remember forever what time it was, where we were, and what we were doing when the unbelievable news reached our ears. Yet most of us continue to live just like we did before 9/11. Nothing, it seems, has changed.

But something has changed. We think and feel differently about ourselves, each other, and our surroundings. Uncertainty, something we Americans are unaccustomed to dealing with, has pervaded our thinking. From the Iraq war to the unemployment picture to the potential for another terror attack, we face an unknown future. Yes, we still have the largest economy and the world's most feared military force. But we are confronted with daunting new forces, some of which we cannot see: forces of the mind.

Although invisible to many, an undeniable undercurrent of negativism and fear has taken root. And it will lead us into a great depression far deeper than the historical depression of the 1930s that is highlighted in our school textbooks.

Actually, this undercurrent was planted not on 9/11, but rather in January and March of 2000. That's when the Dow Jones and NASDAQ stock price indices ended the longest bull market in United States history. At that point, we entered a two-and-a-half-year bear market most people believe bottomed out October 10, 2002. As of August 2005, many are convinced that we are now in a new bull market and that investors will recoup all their losses.

But there's a problem: The same patterns and trends of early 2000 have returned. From August 2004 through July 2005 investors once again pumped billions of dollars into mutual funds. A large number of investors bought stocks on margin just as they did in early 2000. Insiders, company presidents and chief executive officers, sold millions of their own company's stock. Furthermore, what could be a sign that cash will soon be king, several major U.S. corporations are sitting on billions of dollars of the green back. As of this writing, it appears that most indices are beginning to roll over, ever so slowly. It is as if the bear wants to get all of the bullish investors, not just most of them.

So what, you ask, does the stock market have to do with the way people feel and think, the American psyche? The answer is: a whole lot.

Billions of transactions occur every day on the New York Stock Exchange and in other markets around the globe. Investors make decisions every day that result in billions of dollars changing hands. And emotions play a major role in those decisions. When emotions such as greed and fear reign, markets behave wildly. We create manias, or bubbles, such as those of 1925–29 and 1995–2000, when greed is king. We create stock market crashes, such as in 1929–32 and 1987, when fear rules. Obviously, these two states of mind and their consequential behavior patterns are not healthy for the markets or the economy.

The American psyche will become even more pessimistic as markets track downward and the bear persists. Watch closely as the numbers drop. At some point, the Dow Jones low of 7181.47 set October 10, 2002, will be taken out. It will either happen abruptly, some time in 2006 or 2007, or it will occur gradually, by 2010. If the former occurs, that is a crash, we will all witness a panic not seen since 1929. Most will not see the signs until it is too late. Some — primarily insiders —will sell stocks early. But most of us will stay in the market too long and lose most of our money, if not all.

Once the Dow Jones index tracks below the 2002 low, you can be sure the downward spiral has begun in earnest. Americans will go through an array of emotions. First there will be surprise.

Then we will see disbelief, shock, concern, fear, frustration, anger, outrage and, finally, depression. These emotions will trigger massive protests and marches in our nation's largest cities. Unemployment will rise sharply. We will have record numbers of real estate foreclosures, and personal and corporate bankruptcies.

And the man in the White House will have no choice but to endure the wrath of angry Americans, who will not care who won the last election, no matter what their political stripes. During the last major depression, incumbent President Hoover was booted out in a landslide that swept Franklin Delano Roosevelt into office. Towns with throngs of the unemployed and homeless were dubbed "Hoovervilles." So could be the destiny of President Bush. Look for "Bushtowns" to spring up everywhere if the depression starts under his watch.

Besides those unseen forces of the mind, there are dangerous visible forces to contend with. Thanks to our president, we have new enemies all over the world. The number of countries whose leaders and people dislike us is on the rise. They are fed up with America's greed, gluttony, and arrogance. We are seen as the spoiled bully. Because of our pride, dangerous forces want what we have—and are determined to take it from us.

Why Booms and Crashes?

In looking back at our nearly 230-year history, several questions come to mind. Why has the United States had several booms and crashes? And what happens when amateurs become involved with these booms? Obviously, the answers are always clearer after bubbles burst. Ninety-nine percent of the population did not expect anything like the stock market crash in 1929 and depression that stung this country in the 1930s. Similarly, the vast majority of people today expect the stock market and economy to keep on rising and expanding. And so, most will be caught off guard and won't even know what hit them. It will be like the frog in the pan of water on the stove. As the temperature rises to the boiling point, the frog does not realize it's in danger until it is too late. And like the deer caught in the glare of headlights, most of us will have no idea which way to turn.

During the Roaring Twenties, investors— including amateurs—were making easy money hand over fist by playing the stock market. Then came the crash of 1929 and the deepest depression in U.S. history. Modern investors say nothing like that will happen anytime soon, either because we already have seen the big crash of our generation or because a 1929-style crash is simply no longer possible. But that is precisely why it *will* happen.

As noted earlier, stock indices are slowly turning over. If this downward trend continues, an economic contraction will begin and several corporations will find it extremely difficult to keep pace with Wall Street's expectations. But why are we again repeating 1929 and 2000? Perhaps a quote from Scottish writer Charles Mackay, who was the author of *Extraordinary Popular Delusions and the Madness in Crowds*, can shed some light. He writes, "Men, it has been well said, think in herds; it will be seen that they go mad in herds, while they recover their senses slowly, and one by one."[1]

Americans love winners

Americans love teams that win. That is why for many years the Dallas Cowboys of the National Football League were known as America's Team. In the 1990s, the Cowboys won three Super Bowls in four years. It also is why millions who rarely watch a baseball game tuned in to see if the Boston Red Sox would win a World Series for the first time in 86 years. When the Red Sox did, 3.2 million fans turned out for the victory parade. They wanted to show appreciation for their team. But perhaps more than that, they wanted to see the team that reversed the curse.

In short, Americans love to jump on the bandwagon. However, when it comes to investing, climbing aboard is not such a good idea at the end of the trail.

When a large number of people, particularly novices, become involved with stock investment clubs or speculate in real estate, it's time to flee such investments. It's never a good sign for any investment vehicle when amateurs get involved. When housing prices soar as fast and as high as they have been, it may seem like just about anyone can get rich in real estate. Those that are buying property now are simply blinded by the $$ signs in their eyes. All of us very soon will see that the numerous get-rich-quick real estate commercials on TV and radio these past few years were actually signaling the end of the housing bubble.

The re-inflated stock market and the red-hot real estate market are about to collapse. Home prices haven't seen a correction in 10 years. In fact, real estate prices decade to decade haven't declined since the 1930s. And the mercurial rise as of late is not a healthy sign for the future because droves of non-experts are buying homes as investments. People are taking advantage of the lowest mortgage interest rates in 40 years. And why shouldn't they? It's easy money courtesy of the United States government. Besides, everyone knows someone who has cashed in on an equity windfall. Many are convinced they must climb aboard this bandwagon now or they will miss out.

A Change is Coming

Unfortunately, this kind of runaway real estate

speculation is causing a herding effect. People are rushing to buy houses before interest rates creep back up and home prices shoot up even more. Just like a herd of stampeding cattle with no sense of direction, buyers are becoming more and more irrational in their thinking. Most don't care at all about the historically high prices. They just want a home. In the case of investment property or a vacation home, many home owners are not concerned if they have a renter or not. These real estate investors are just banking on the continuing property value appreciation. Also, prospective buyers are so desperate for "ownership" that they are willing to sign 40-year or interest-only mortgages. The sad reality is, these unfortunate people will be the first to turn their keys in to their bank.

As for stock investors, they will grow increasingly anxious as markets continue their downward trend, and they will begin selling in earnest. The Dow Jones' inability to stay above 10,000 will be the first alarm. Then more worry and fear will spread like gangrene as the Dow Jones begins to flail, falling below 9000 initially, then 8000. Once the 7000 mark is breached, the herding phenomenon will start to reverse as both the stock market and real estate bubbles begin to pop. As Robert Prechter explains in his book *The Wave Principle of Human Social Behavior and the New Science of Socionomics*, "The error of optimism dies and gives birth to an error of pessimism."[2] This psychology is the primary ingredient of booms and crashes.

Stock advisors and brokers are so confused with today's market activity they don't really know what to tell clients. Unknowingly, some have forecasted incorrect tops and bottoms. One in particular advised a national radio audience to buy stocks, as he had predicted a summer 2004 rally he thought would begin in July. Instead, the stock market plummeted to a low in August 2004. A short time before this low, he told listeners to sell everything and buy oil stocks. In November, the market once again exploded, reaching another high in what was called the Bush rally. That led this advisor to suggest a new bull market had arrived. At every turn this advisor was wrong. When he urged clients to buy, they would have been better off selling, and vice versa.

Essentially, the Bush rally was a panic-buy rally that caused markets to rise quickly. It took the rally just three weeks to wipe out eight months' of losses. But the Bush rally was really just another sign of irrational behavior.

Just like the beyond-reason buying frenzy in the real estate market, we are about to see a selling panic in the stock market. This will have an effect on everyone. And the downside to the herding effect will have bred a downward spiral of negativity, fear and despair.

The American psyche is clearly headed in the wrong direction. To turn us around, America will need a leader like Abraham Lincoln, who led this country to victory in the bloody Civil War and helped abolish slavery. The United States will need a leader like Franklin Roosevelt, who united this nation and helped Americans weather the Great Depression with his famous fireside chats. Together we will overcome. Together we will regain that spirit of unity, like we did in the days following 9/11. When America hits bottom, we must come to our senses one by one and ask God for help like we did on Sept. 11, 2001.

Simpler Times Please

Countless times in my early years, while growing up on my family's dairy farm in Iowa, I would ponder how fortunate I was to live in a nation that provided so much freedom and opportunity. I remember spending countless hours day-dreaming about my future. I wanted to be a professional football player or the first person to walk on the red planet, Mars. There were two reasons for that. My favorite football team, the Green Bay Packers, had just won the first two Super Bowls. And the United States had just put the first man on the moon.

The year was 1969. I was 12 years old. Life was simple, especially for a boy on a Midwest farm. No one was in a hurry. And if you met someone on a gravel road you always waved, no matter who it was—neighbor, friend, or total stranger.

Almost everyone was a Sunday driver. Traveling from Garden Grove to Dallas Center to visit Grandma seemed to take forever. It didn't help that my older sisters bored me to death, counting horses as we drove Highways 69 and 6, and Interstate 35. Iowa, with its lush green vegetation and beautiful rolling hills, was truly the best place in the world to grow up. Life was so simple, so easygoing.

My parents were as conservative as you could get, as they themselves were raised during the Great Depression. The lessons they learned from their parents they passed on to my three sisters and me. However, over time those lessons became harder to remember and harder to implement. I do remember, though, in the late 70s, while attending electronic school in West Des Moines, Iowa, and working part time, that I could save at least half my paycheck.

Life is so very different now—so complex and so difficult. Most of us feel like a metal ball in a pinball machine that is bounced all over the place, without any control of its own. Our jobs are like that. The demands we face seem to become more complex by the day. For many Americans, our homes have become a place only to rest for the night, rather than a place for spending an evening with a warm family where members express genuine concern for each other. Where has the communication gone? Where have all the flowers gone?

Because of the 2000-2002 bear market and today's uncertain economy, businesses throughout the United States are taking great pains to cut costs in every department. To make sure each department is performing at its highest possible level, managers are working longer hours to keep up with demands coming down from the top. As for the rest of us —the ones who actually do the work—we are doing three to four times what we did just three years ago. And more often than not, we're not getting any special training for that extra workload.

If we do receive training, it is done in an hour instead of three hours. If a test is given at the end of the class, sometimes the trainer is forced to give out answers because the information is too complex to comprehend in the time available. E-mails come from as many as 25 different departments. In order to keep up with this required knowledge, sometimes we have to read them on our own time. If our position involves communicating with customers, we are required to say exactly what our company wants us to. There might be as many as ten required statements. If we don't say them all, we are "dinged." Every "t" must be crossed and every "i" dotted. This is called productivity. Because of this added workload, life on the job has become infinitely more complicated and stressful.

As of this writing, the economy is struggling

to keep its gains of the last two and a half years. Company budgets will become extremely tight, forcing companies to layoff those that they may have just hired. Many companies will demand the remaining employees to do more and more work. Some employees love to be pushed this way, but the majority will get burned out and quit. Or they will eventually fight back and say enough is enough.

However, as jobs become more scarce, employers will have the upper hand. As the economy begins to weaken over the next few years, most companies will be forced to squeeze still more productivity out of their current employees. Employees will have to adapt to still more demands. As the economy continues to weaken, companies will find it increasingly difficult to curb costs. Eventually, firms will be forced to ax jobs in huge numbers.

For that reason, your biggest asset is how well you do your job and how valuable you are to your employer. Be the best of the best. Give your boss many reasons for keeping you and zero for letting you go. Hang in there. It is better to persevere under an ever-increasing workload than to struggle financially while looking for another way to put food on the table.

So just why is today's world so complex? Will we ever get back to simpler times? Of course, there are several reasons why we live in a complex world. The main reason is at our fingertips. It is the computer. Because of the computer and the

Internet, we have far more information available to us than at any other time in history. Innovation and technology keep delivering faster and smarter computers, which in turn deliver information at ever-increasing speeds. The computer also has provided a way for businesses to cut costs by going paperless, relying solely on systems to provide all the information an employee needs to do his or her job through the click of a mouse.

It sounds simple, but only for those who can keep up. We have become overloaded with information. Therefore, I predict the expansion of the information age is about to run its course. Since technology is directly tied to information, the information age will dramatically wind down in the coming years.

How do I know this, you ask? Well, consider this. When we have companies and other various corporations reporting higher product inventories due to lower consumer spending, we have the beginnings of a business contraction. And that means lower profits. When businesses contract, every department gets its budget slashed, including the crucial research and development division. Less money in turn translates into less innovation and, in some cases, none at all. And less innovation means less information.

The world that we know is about to change forever. Some of us will want something major to happen to wake us up. From crooked politicians to cooked corporate books to complicated job demands, Americans are about to say, "Enough is enough. We've had enough of this fast-paced, complicated, stressed-out world."

Sooner or later we will get our way. Indeed, two to three years from now, we may not recognize this country. The United States is on the verge of waking up to what really matters. For many of us, life will be reduced to having a job that pays only for clothes on our backs, food on our tables, and roofs over our heads. For many, having a job that just takes care of the bare necessities will be considered a tremendous blessing. For many of us, a steady income will no longer be the trigger for ever-increasing greed but rather the difference between simply having a home and being homeless.

So what is wrong with America's psyche? Will we ever get back to simpler times, when we didn't have to think so much and when life wasn't so stressful? Will America survive the worldwide pessimistic trend that began in 2000 and 2001?

I truly hope America will survive the next great depression and experience a time like the 1950s when almost everyone was a Sunday driver.

Chapter 3

The Causes of the Next Great Depression

As in the Great Depression of the 1930s, Americans will be clamoring to know why and how another depression happened. We will have tons of questions, but few answers. We will have many opinions, but few will make sense.

In my opinion, the causes of the next great depression will be clear: An unseen reversal in psychology from optimism to pessimism was the catalyst to a bear market in stock exchanges in 2000. Basic economics and common sense were abandoned as government leaders, in their insatiable thirst for power, ignored the warning signals of the largest national and personal debt in history and an extreme over-extension of credit. The bursting of the credit bubble, along with the crash of the stock and housing markets, ushered in fears of deflation and a contracting economy, which produced a downward spiral of despair and the greatest U.S. depression of all time.

The American Debt

It doesn't take a rocket scientist to realize America has a bad spending habit. According to the Bureau of the Public Debt in April 2005, the federal debt stood at $7.8 trillion—an increase of $1.8 trillion since President Bush took office.[1]

As if that weren't enough, total personal debt had skyrocketed to $10.3 trillion, as of that same month.[2] That figure includes $803.5 billion of revolving credit and $1.3 trillion of non-revolving credit as well as $8.2 trillion in mortgage debt. Meanwhile, corporate debt has soared above $7.8 trillion for the first time.[3] And, of course, our federal government is setting the pace for all of us in 2005. A report from the Congressional Budget Office indicated the federal government had a record deficit for a single month of $113.9 billion in February. Also, the CBO is projecting a 2005 federal deficit of $394 billion.[4]

All this adds up to a record U.S. debt of somewhere between $37 trillion and $84 trillion, depending on what debts you include. But any way you slice it, the United States has become the single largest debtor in the world.

But it's not just the sheer magnitude of our debt that is alarming. It's also disturbing how fast we are plunging ever deeper into the red. In just one year—2004—household debt shot up 4.8 percent, climbing to $2.1 trillion.[5] Likewise from 2002 to 2004 a total of $9.09 trillion dollars of mortgage loans were funded by the nation's mortgage bankers.[6] Making things worse, personal bankruptcies have been rising over the last 10 years with an all-time record of 1,613,097 filings for the fiscal year ending June 30, 2003. Even though 2004 produced an economic expansion, personal bankruptcies were only 13,111 lower, with a total of 1,599,986 filings for the year ending June 30, 2004.[7]

We don't have to look far to see where all this is going. On January 12, 2004, William Branigin of the *Washington Post* stated in an article that, "To some, the nation's consumer debt, which dwarfs that of any other country, represents the kind of 'bubble' that the stock market grew into during the 1990s."[8] Mr. Branigin also mentioned that the credit-card industry estimated the average household credit-card balance at $9,000. Then if you figure that 40 percent of all credit-card holders pay off monthly balances, the total amount of credit-card balance for the remaining 60 percent is more like $13,000 per household.

America, we have a problem. Why are we spending money we don't even have? What's the point of keeping up with the Joneses if we don't have a dime to our name?

The Greenspan Bluff

Now, if you ask Federal Reserve Chairman Alan Greenspan what he thinks about all this debt, you get conflicting answers. Take, for example, a quote from a speech he delivered to the Economic Club of New York on March 2, 2004: "Can market forces incrementally defuse a worrisome buildup in a nation's current account deficit and net external debt before a crisis more abruptly does so?"[9] True, Mr. Greenspan did not specify that he was talking about the United States, but it sure seemed like he was. After all, we are the largest debtor nation in the world. However, in a speech to the Credit Union National Association a couple of days later, he suggested there is no threat of crisis as he stated, "Overall, the household sector seems to be in good shape."[10]

After reading this last quote, it would appear that Mr. Greenspan found a solution to all this debt. Or rather that he found the necessary trillions of dollars to fix the imbalances: consumer debt and the federal budget deficit. Sorry to say, Mr. Greenspan did not. However, he is still trying to convince us not to worry. On Oct. 26, 2004, before an organization called America's Community Bankers, Mr. Greenspan said, "Household finances appear to be in reasonably good shape."[11] On the other hand, he did suggest things could change if there is a sharp decline in housing prices and consumer paychecks. Mr. Greenspan is hoping you don't read between the lines. He and President Bush want the American public to believe everything is okay. Unfortunately, Mr. Greenspan, like the second-term Republican president, will be saddled with the dubious distinction of having started the next depression. That label will follow him even after he steps down from chairmanship of the Federal Reserve come early 2006.

The Housing Bubble

Over the last three years, I have come to realize the economy lags behind the stock market four to twelve months. For example, when markets peaked in January and March of 2000, the mini-recession that followed did not get underway until January 2001. Likewise, the economic expansion we've enjoyed since late 2003 began after markets hit a temporary bottom in October 2002.

Real estate prices typically start to fall two to three years after a major top in the stock market. This occurred in the 1930s, then again in 1989. However, real estate prices have continued to climb steeply because of the low interest rates and expanding credit bubble, courtesy of Mr. Greenspan and the Federal Reserve. But how long will it all last? It depends on when the credit bubble begins to lose air. Unfortunately, the longer the credit bubble lasts, the more dramatic the collapse will be.

We have all known since we were children that what goes up must come down. As simple as that sounds, the very same principle applies to the stock and housing markets. Yet it is disturbing that we haven't seen a healthy correction in real estate prices for some time, in fact more than a decade. Not only have prices continued to climb, this rise has fueled the same kind of speculation in the real estate arena that we saw in the stock market in the late 1990s. A March 2004 report by Bridgewater Associates, a money manager and institutional research firm from Connecticut, illustrates this genuine concern with the real estate bubble: "As with any unsustainable market, or economic event, it is impossible to pinpoint when the reversal is about to take place, but a pop in this bubble will likely have a larger affect on households than the popping of the NASDAQ did."[12] Furthermore, an article by Tom Kelly of STLtoday.com shows how much speculation is actually in the real estate market. An online survey by the National Association of Realtors revealed "that 23 percent of all homes purchased in 2004 were for investment, while another 13 percent were vacation homes," Mr Kelly continued. "It now appears that the purchase of investment property and vacation homes accounts for more than one-third of residential transactions."[13]

It is interesting to note that, from 1995 to 2000, when the stock market was in its heyday, the NASDAQ climbed 44 percent per year. Similarly, since March of 2000, the stocks of homebuilders have soared 46 percent each year.[14]

Furthermore, when investors lost money in the bear market of March 2000 to October 2002, many invested what they had left in real estate. This infusion of new money spurred prices to rise even higher. According to a report released in July 2005 by the California Association of Realtors (C.A.R.), the median price for a single family home in California was $542,720 in June.[15] In July 2005, C.A.R. reported the affordability index, a percentage of households that can afford to purchase a median priced home, slid in May to 16 percent, a drop of 3 percent from a year ago. Obviously, with these outrageous prices many Americans are not able to buy a house.

Looking at U.S. Census reports for the last two decades, median home values for the nation as a whole increased by an average of 28 percent from 1980 ($93,400) to 2000 ($119,600).[16] Since 1940, there has never been a decade in which median prices dropped. We have to go all the way back to 1930 to find such a major correction in the real estate market.

Now, let's fast forward to 2005. In June 2005, the national median existing-home price was $217,000, a stunning 81.5 percent increase since just the turn of the century.[17] It has taken a mere five years for prices to blaze well past the rate of increase for the previous 20 years. The bottom line is, this trend simply cannot be sustained much longer.

In regards to local markets, Mr Greenspan seems to agree. On June 9, 2005, Mr. Greenspan testified before the Joint Economic Committee of Congress that, "Although a 'bubble' in home prices for the nation as a whole does not appear likely, there do appear to be, at a minimum, signs of froth in some local markets where home prices seem to have risen to unsustainable levels." But what do you call a 81.5 percent leap in the national median existing-home price in five years compared to a much more gradual 28 percent rise over two decades? You call it what it is—a *nation-wide* real estate bubble that will burst within two or three years. In fact, the decline of real estate prices will be like climbing down Mt. Everest without any ropes or picks and via a descent that has never been attempted before. In others words a free-fall.

Of course, it didn't help that President Bush, in several 2004 campaign speeches, urged Americans to continue buying homes. He even promised some could achieve home ownership with no money down.[18] Ownership plus no money down equals bank-owned to me. Furthermore, we all know what our president's spending habits are like and how they have produced record deficits. And now he is encouraging us to take on still more debt.

I've got a question for you, Mr. President. When will all these bills be paid? The truth is, most will go unpaid. Many "home owners" will default on their loans and turn in their keys to the bank. As interest rates surge higher, Americans will no longer be able to refinance their mortgages. And the resulting spending freeze will trigger the end of the real estate bubble.

It is very clear why President Bush is pushing ownership. The housing industry and some would say the war in Iraq have kept this economy moving. And he knows it. Bush knows that when Americans stop buying homes and refinancing mortgages, they will also stop running down to Home Depot and Ikea to buy things for those new houses. Remember, we the people are 70 percent of the economy. And President Bush is determined to keep us spending.

What the president doesn't seem to understand is that he is only pumping more air into the bubble. This bubble is becoming so huge that, when it finally bursts, real estate prices are going to plummet 60 percent to 90 percent in the coming deflation. And it's not like something similar hasn't happened before. Consider a case in point: In 1836, an acre of land in Chicago was fetching $11,000. By 1840, that same acre was being given away for a mere $100.[19] And again, we cannot forget that the real estate market has not had a substantial correction in more than 75 years.

Certainly, it is hard to believe that a house valued at $200,000 today could be worth only $20,000 some three or four years from now. But if history repeats itself, as I strongly believe it will, we will witness a precipitous drop in home prices. I'm not going to tell you to sell. But if you choose not to sell, prepare to be upside down for the entire period covered by your mortgage, and be sure to keep the house for the rest of your life so you can *give* it to one of your children when you pass away.

The approaching winter will so shake our confidence that many of us will begin to realize there is more to life than climbing to the top of the corporate ladder, living in the biggest house on the block, and collecting the most toys. Many of us will desire a return to the values of the noble men and women that shaped this great country and won our independence in the late 1700s.

The Start of the Credit Bubble's Collapse

In the book *Conquer the Crash*, author Robert R. Prechter, Jr. says the collapse of the credit bubble must be preceded by a huge buildup in the extension of credit. We are talking about bank loans, corporate and consumer debt, credit card debt, and home mortgages. Mr. Prechter says, "Near the end of a major expansion, few creditors expect default, which is why they lend freely to weak borrowers. Few borrowers expect their fortunes to change, which is why they borrow freely." However, as Mr. Prechter continues, "The expansion of credit ends when the desire or ability to sustain the trend can no longer be maintained."[20] In other words, the lender stops lending because the borrower doesn't have the cash to pay back loans. And once the credit bubble starts to lose air, consumers will no longer have cash for buying appliances, furniture, equipment, cars, and houses. Simply put, consumers will stop consuming. As the winds of deflation begin to blow, cash again will become king as consumers sell assets to pay debts.

Clearly, within the next year or two, Americans will grow a lot less confident about the stock market and overall economy. Many of us will actually start spending our money more wisely. Most of the things we buy will be what we need and not what we want. It won't be long before we are able to relate to cowboy comedian Will Rogers. In the book *Reflections and Observations* in 1932, Mr. Rogers mused, "Gosh, wasn't we crazy there for a while? Why the thought never entered our head that we wasn't the brightest, wisest, and the most accomplished people that was ever on this earth. Hadn't we figured out 'mass production'? Couldn't we make more things than anybody? Did the thought ever enter our bone head that the time might come when nobody would want all these things we were making? No, we had it all figured out that the more we made, the more they would want. Honest, as we look back now, somebody ought to have taken each one of us and soaked our fat heads. We bought everything under the sun, if they would sell it on enough installments."[21]

Back in the 1920s, consumers bought merchandise by making monthly payments called installments. The longer the period covered by the installments, the more you could buy. Of course, today we have credit cards and various types of loans. Against the backdrop of the lowest interest rates in 40 years, consumers are bombarded weekly with offers to apply for credit cards. However, the spending spree is just about over. The time is coming when we will all start spending a lot less. Unfortunately, this decrease in spending will usher in the most feared of all economic conditions: deflation. And because consumer spending accounts for 70 percent of our nation's economy, the credit bubble will burst. Remember, credit does not equal cash; credit equals debt. The bubble of easy money is like a volcano that's ready to blow its top.

So, do Mr. Greenspan and President Bush realize that a very long and bitter economic winter is upon us? Obviously, our leaders are highly educated and determined to do the best job that they can. But, given that they are among the smartest people in the world, shouldn't Bush and Greenspan be able to see the major imbalances and bubbles that are occurring? It is not clear whether they know— however, even if they do know, they can't do anything about it. Raising and lowering interest rates won't do any good when the gigantic, hideous monster of debt cries out, "Pay now!" The damage has already been done. The only hope our leaders have of staving off the burst is to keep the American public confident for as long as possible. But our confidence is on thin ice and a large number of Americans will be forced to endure a long and bitterly cold economic winter.

It's Up to the Consumer

Years from now, when we look back on the causes of the Greatest Depression of all time, we will see that we consumers did exactly what our government wanted us to do. We shopped until we dropped. We did as much as we could. Instead of charging four credit cards, we applied for four more. Instead of saving for a rainy day, we bought a new truck, a new entertainment system or a new house. Some of us bought a second house for investment purposes, believing that what went up would keep going up. Not to mention that President Bush encouraged us to do all this. He doled out tax refunds and gave us the opportunity to spend more of our money. Meanwhile, he and the Federal Reserve slashed the overnight interest rate to 1 percent, the lowest in 40 years. And his very own shop-until-you-drop example left us with a terribly unbalanced government checkbook.

The Bush administration, all on its own, has managed to wipe out trillions of dollars of surplus. Will President Bush ever balance the checkbook? Not on President Bush's watch. With a $400 billion projected 2005 deficit, he certainly shows no intention of bringing things back into balance. And with the credit bubble just about to burst and Americans fast running out of cash to buy tomorrow's junk, deflation is about to rise from the dead after a 75-year absence. It is only a matter of time.

Deflation's Return

On April 20, 2004, Alan Greenspan said the "D" word. Yes, he muttered the word that is feared and dreaded in economic circles: Deflation. In testifying on Capitol Hill, Greenspan said, "It's fairly apparent that pricing power is gradually being restored and... threats of deflation, which were a significant concern last year, by all indications are no longer an issue before us."[22] One year earlier, he didn't have the stomach to say the word. On May 21, 2003, Mr. Greenspan spoke rather of an "unwelcome substantial fall in inflation."[23] Why is Mr. Greenspan so comfortable saying the word deflation now? Because he managed to re-inflate the economy since mid-2003. However, Greenspan's future replacement and President Bush are between a rock and a hard place. They are going to have to make a choice between deflation and inflation. They are in a Catch-22. If they raise interest rates to combat inflation, the economy may stall and abruptly halt America's spending spree. If they choose not to increase rates, the economy may overheat and trigger the kind of double-digit inflation that dogged America in the 1970s. This could cause the credit and housing bubble to bulge even more, portending only more and bigger problems down the road. So what are we going to see? Inflation or deflation?

There are many opinions out there about this, and certainly everyone is entitled to one. But not everyone will be right. Most will be wrong. The problem is, most people get their opinions from the national news media, a market guru on television, or their own belief system. Most are convinced we will never see a market or economic collapse on the scale of the Great Depression and that our government has the means to keep us from going down that road again. However, I choose to base my opinion on research and the notion that people tend to repeat history—especially when we don't learn from past mistakes. It is amazing that most people view the 1990s and early 2000s as a repeat of the 1920s, yet hardly anyone expects something like the conditions of the 1930s to follow anytime soon, if ever.

Over the next several months the markets will begin the first stages of uncertainty, which will eventually turn into a sense of fear and panic. The idea that the Dow Jones could fall below 7,181 is the farthest thing from people's minds. But if you examine the Dow from 2000 to 2005, there's a downward trend that will take the Dow below 5,500 and lower. (Go to http://www.geocities.

com/theapproachingwinter for the 1929-1932 and 2000-2005 Dow Jones downward charts). The bear market is about to begin again.

Why am I talking, you ask, about the markets when the subject is deflation? Because they are an indicator of what is to come. Remember, the markets lead the economy. A long bear market rally has managed to push prices up from early 2003 to 2005. This rally re-inflated the economy with a lot of help from sharply rising oil prices. But once markets resume their downward trend, deflation will not be far behind. Americans' prosperity is linked to the stock market more today than at any time in our nation's history. Huge numbers of workers, particularly those in the private sector, depend on 401(k) plans or IRAs for retirement. Those individual retirement accounts give us the opportunity to invest in our employers' stock, the stock of other companies, or various mutual funds. So, when market prices fall over a long period, March 2000 to October 2002, we become concerned about our future. If the troubling trend continues, we start cutting back and look for ways to save. This mind-set, which economists call self preservation, is what actually triggers the downward spiral of deflation. Look for even petroleum and gold to decline, even though crude oil prices have surged above $60 per barrel and gold prices have reached as high as $460 an ounce. In fact, all commodity prices will deflate by 60 percent to 90 percent from their current peaks.

Why will prices fall? The answer lies in Basic Economics 101 and the most fundamental of economic theories: supply and demand. As consumers cut back on their spending, demand will decrease, lowering prices. In turn, this will trigger an oversupply of products, driving down prices more. As the downward trend gains a foothold, look for several department and novelty store chains to file for bankruptcy and close their doors. That will leave still more products on the shelf, reducing prices even more.

You may be skeptical of all this. You may be thinking that consumers are just not going to cut back so sharply on their spending, triggering all these other negative trends. After all, we love to spend our money. But you can spend what you don't have for only so long. And many consumers will be forced to cut back because of their tremendous debt load. Then, unfortunately, when the debt bubble begins to explode, the housing market will come crashing down, causing many Americans to be upside down in their mortgages.

We must not forget that a large number of businesses are linked to the housing industry. Consider, for a moment, all the different trades that play a role in the building of a home. There must be more than 100 types of businesses that get involved in some way. Working for all those businesses are millions of people who will lose their jobs very quickly when the bubble bursts.

Once interest rates start rising the refinance fountain will run dry. Millions of Americans are living paycheck to paycheck. If we stop spending, companies will have to cut expenses by slashing wages or laying people off, or both. This, too, will cause deflation to come roaring back.

Deflation is very foreign to us. The last time it occurred was during the Great Depression. And it lasted only a few years. It always requires a credit bubble like the one we have today and a government that tries too hard to control it.

It always ends in disaster. It is twice as bad as inflation. Indeed, it was deflation that was behind the depression of the 1930s, while inflation was behind the recession of the 1970s. Once America starts cutting back on her spending binge, it will be interesting to see whether Mr. Greenspan, or his replacement, has the stomach to say "deflation"!

Chapter 4

Winter's Fury

Winters in Iowa can be mild, with only a little snow. Or they can be stormy and bitterly cold, sparing no one from their icy fury. I remember that working on the farm in winter was extremely difficult. Even getting out of bed was a struggle, as my family lived in a house with two wood-burning stoves and no running water.

To keep warm at night, we slept between a pair of flannel sheets with three or four covers. When we awoke and rolled out of bed, our feet would feel like icicles as we touched down on the nearly frozen floor and scampered downstairs. We made a beeline for the stoves, warming our front sides first and forcing our backs to wait their turn to thaw out. Then we'd switch sides. The moment we did, our front sides would start to freeze again.

I never did like the cold, and that is one reason I don't live in Iowa anymore. Just thinking about those nights and days when temperatures stayed below zero gives me the chills.

Surviving those frosty Midwest winters required toughness and the ability to endure adversity. Those same qualities will prove to be crucial for all Americans in the coming years, as the country plunges headlong toward an economic winter: the next great depression. It unfortunately—and undoubtedly—will be prove to be the worst economic crisis of all time.

The seven to twenty years of despair that are about to wash over this nation like a tsunami will not be mild and will affect every man, woman, and child. Almost every American will be hammered by the crash of the stock and housing markets, which will trigger the loss of millions of jobs. As the voices of the late 1990s cried, "Prosperity for everyone," so those voices will cry out despair for everyone. As the forces of deflation tighten their icy grip on the United States, an economic winter will arrive.

The Great Depression of the Thirties

To catch a glimpse of the next great depression, we need to revisit the last one. Numerous books have been written on the subject of the Great Depression; about what started it, the people who endured it, and why recovery was so slow in coming.

What's amazing is that, three-quarters of a century later, economists and historians are still debating what caused the historic stock market crash of 1929 and the Great Depression of the 1930s, and whether those events were connected. Some scholars actually believe there was no connection between the crash and the hard times that followed. It's not a good sign when the smartest people in the world can't figure that out. Unfortunately, we are destined to repeat history precisely because scholars are clueless about an event that dramatically changed this country and was so defining that it closed out one era and started another!

The Calm Before the Storm

In the book *Rainbow's End: The Crash of 1929*, author Maury Klein writes about several individuals who helped shape the crash and depression. One was President Herbert Hoover, who was fingered more than anyone else for the hard times. Another was Benjamin Strong, who, as governor of the New York Federal Reserve Bank, became the most influential member of the Federal Reserve System.

Klein shines a different light on Hoover, providing us insight into the former president's views regarding the stock market in the mid-1920s. "Unlike many priests of the New Era, however, Hoover did not bask in the glow of the steadily rising stock market," Klein writes. "He had long opposed what he called the 'growing tide of speculation' and as early as 1925 had urged Adolph Miller of the Federal Reserve Board to restrict credit. Three times in 1926, beginning on New Year's Day, Hoover warned against 'real estate and stock speculation and its possible extension into commodities with inevitable inflation, the over extension of installment buying' and similar perils. 'Psychology plays a large part in the business movements,' he added, 'and optimism can only land us on the shores of depression.'"[1] Little did Hoover know his own words would come back to haunt him four years later. As the economy continued to expand into 1928, Hoover declared during his campaign for the Republican Party's nomination for president that America was headed for even more prosperity. Nothing advanced the notion more that the nation was headed for good times than Herbert Hoover's acceptance speech later that year. In that address, he stated: "We in America today are nearer to the final triumph over poverty than ever before in the history of any land. The poor house is vanishing from among us. We have not yet reached the goal, but given a chance to go forward with the policies of the last eight years, and we shall soon, with the help of God, be in sight of the day when poverty will be banished from this nation."[2]

As we all know, it didn't turn out that way. Instead of more good times, a depression got underway in mid-1930 and it persisted through 1937. It delivered seven-plus years of poverty for several million Americans, as more than 13 million citizens were jobless. Thirty percent of Americans were unemployed. And it left Hoover with anything but a flattering legacy. He was in the wrong place at the wrong time. And as people repeat history, President Bush may inherit a similar legacy.

Klein also writes about Strong, who actually died before the depression in October 1928. However, before his death, Strong sounded some alarm bells. He wasn't concerned so much about the "easy money" policy as he was about the nation's prevailing attitude. "I do not think the problem is necessarily one of security prices or of available volume of credit, or even of discount rates," Strong wrote in one of his letters. "It is really a problem of psychology. The country's state of mind has been highly speculative, advancing prices have been based upon a realization of wealth and prosperity;… consequently speculative tendencies are all the more difficult to deal with… The problem now is so to shape our policy as to avoid a calamitous break in the stock market, a panicky feeling about money, a setback to business because of the change in psychology."[3]

This same state of mind is the key to our future. As we mentioned in Chapter 2, the rising stock market prices of 2003 and 2004 and the increasing paper wealth homeowners are enjoying has kept this negative psychology at bay for now. However, the more talk we hear about a New Era or New Economy, and about booms without crashes, the more people will be willing to risk. The more investors we have out there who believe the Dow Jones will just keep on climbing to, say, 36,000 or higher, the more people will invest. The "realization of wealth and prosperity" has given increasingly more people the opportunity to speculate in the stock market and real estate. And as a result, expectations are extremely high. There soon will come a time, however, when investors will stop buying stocks and start selling them in earnest. As of July 2005, we were at a period in history called the calm before the storm. We are talking about a period when the weather is sunny and warm, and there appears to be no threat of a storm, and yet a killer hurricane is only hours away.

The summer of 1929 was just such a time of sunny and warm days, when it came to both the weather and economy. The economy was purring along like a well-oiled engine with no breakdown in sight. The high-flying automobile industry was doing particularly well.

In the book *The Hungry Years*, author T. H. Watkins writes, "Ford was hardly free of competitors. There were forty-four other automobile-makers in business by 1929, although the big three of Ford, General Motors and Chrysler were responsible for the manufacture and sale of more than 80 percent of the nearly 4.5 million cars built in the United States every year."[4] In August, times were so good, as Klein writes, "Henry Ford watched Model A number 2,000,000 roll off the assembly line less than seven months after number 1,000,000 had made its debut."[5]

The automobile wasn't the only hot item in 1929. Sales of radio and home appliances set records throughout the late Twenties. In the book *The Great Depression*, Robert S. McElvaine writes, "Productivity increased astronomically. Between 1920 and 1929, output per person-hour soared upward by 63 percent. If the economy was to stay afloat, someone had to buy these products. Many of them were new. Starting from a tiny base in 1922, sales of radios had increased by 1,400 percent by 1929. There was a similar, if not quite so spectacular, explosion in sales of such household appliances as vacuum cleaners, electric irons, refrigerators and washing machines. Such new industries helped greatly in producing the economic boom of the decade."[6]

But even though the economy looked good on the outside, its continued health depended on two critical fundamentals: public confidence, and continued spending by the well-to-do. Were either one of these cogs to falter, the economy would slip. Yet industries continued to increase production because everyone thought the economy would just keep on expanding. Business people were convinced that 1930 would turn out to be yet another banner year.

However, the crash of the stock market started a downward spiral in the American psyche and the nation was never the same after that. America's confidence was shattered. Because of this,

Americans started to cut back on their spending to pay off debt. But by then it was too late. The calm before the storm had given way to a category 5 killer hurricane.

The Crash of 1929

They call it Black Tuesday. That's because the worst stock market crash in U.S. history fell on Tuesday, October 29, 1929. Billions of dollars were lost. Millions of lives were ruined. Panic and fear seized investors as 16,410,030 shares changed hands on that historic day. That was even more than the stunning 12,900,000 shares that changed hands just a few days before, on October 24, which came to be known as Black Thursday. Both were the type of days no one forgets. They were stamped forever in people's minds. Most remembered exactly what they were doing, where they were, and what time it was when they heard the shocking and sobering news.

But what caused the stock market to crumble? Probably the unseen change in psychology. Most investors saw the sluggish activity in the month before as a normal correction to the then-all-time closing high of 381.10 recorded on Sept. 3. Also, during the first part of October volume increased to the downside. Signs that something was very wrong should have become obvious on Oct. 21. The Dow declined to 314.55 intra-day. That represented a plunge of more than 17 percent from the record high. And it came with the highest volume—6,090,000 shares—that had been recorded since March 26 of that year. Furthermore, this fall to 314.55 was less than 10 points short of a 20 percent decline, something most economists today define as a bear market.

On Oct. 23, the Dow seemed to stabilize. It peaked at 329.94, some 9 points above the closing on the 21st. However, in her book *Six Days in October: The Stock Market Crash of 1929*, Karen Blumenthal writes, "...in the last hours of trading... stock prices seemed to melt. Out of nowhere, every one dropped a shocking $5 or $15 a share in frantic trading because no one would step up to buy them. More than 2.6 million shares changed hands in the chaotic final hour of trading, as many as might trade in a regular day. When the gong that ended trading rang at 3 p.m., the market was weak and trembling."[7] The intra-day low of 303.84 and the closing at 305.85 could have been the reason for the sell-off in the last hour, as it represented a decline of exactly 20 percent from the record high and signaled the beginning of a bear market.

Unfortunately, that last hour was just the beginning of panic at the New York Stock Exchange. On October 24, the panic selling continued. "Within minutes, prices started to sink, weighted down by a powerful, unseen force... The price declines were eye-popping. General Electric's price slid $25 a share, Westinghouse was down $20, General

Motors fell more than $12. The shares of Auburn Auto, another car maker, had dropped $77 a share on Wednesday. On Thursday, it plunged another $70, to $190. Millions of shares were changing hands as small and large investors tried to preserve something of their winnings and get out. With each drop in price, someone was losing money."[8]

If some wealthy bankers hadn't decided to buy millions of dollars in shares in a last-ditch bid to shore up the market, the carnage would have been worse. After notching an intra-day low of 272.32, the Dow actually closed at 299.47, only 5 points off the previous day's close. But the damage had been done. Investors lost a combined $3 billion.

Bankers wanted President Hoover to issue a statement to try to calm investors and assure the American public that the stock market was stable. But this didn't sit well with Hoover, who in private might have wanted to say, "I told you so," to each and every banker in the country. After all, he had battled Wall Street during the first year of his term. He had tried to slow down the over-speculation that had come to possess the market.

As Blumenthal continues, "To President Hoover, it was an 'orgy of speculation.' Stock prices were too high, he was sure, and the painful declines of October 23 and October 24 were long overdue. Even if he believed this with all his heart, however, on October 25, he had to come up with something more cheerful and reassuring to say publicly to the American people. The president settled on a statement that had all the spice of a bowl of oatmeal: 'The fundamental business of the country, that is production and distribution of commodities, is on a sound and prosperous basis.' The president noted that production and consumption were still at high levels, worker wages and productivity were increasing, and other factors looked good."[9] The president's statement seemed to put the brakes on selling. The Dow added almost 2 points to close at 301.22 on Friday the 25th. Saturday's half day delivered more of the same, as the Dow closed at 298.97. Then came Monday.

Monday turned out to be yet another highly volatile day, as the Dow lost 38 points and closed at 260. The bear market was beginning to awaken. And like a bear that has been away for a long winter's nap, this market was ready for the next kill. The big kill, of course, arrived the following day on what we all know from our history books as Black Tuesday—the worst one-day loss to that time.

In the book *Black Tuesday: The Stock Market Crash of 1929*, author Barbara Silberdick Feinherg writes, "At 10:30 A.M., 650,000 shares of U.S. Steel had been dumped on the market and the stock's price per share plummeted from $205 to $179. During the first six minutes of trading, General Electric stock dropped a dollar every 10 seconds. Westinghouse lost two dollars a minute during the first quarter of an hour... By eleven o'clock, the stocks were being sold for whatever price they could bring... The wave of selling spread quickly. Shareholders all over the United States had flocked to their brokers and watched in disbelief as the tumbling stock prices were posted on chalkboards. The value of their shares continued to drop so they decided to cut their losses."[10] To make things worse, bankers were unwilling to step in to prop up the market.

The day's ending numbers were unbelievable and downright horrific. A record 16,410,000 shares had changed hands. Fourteen billion dollars had vanished into thin air. In less than 60 days, the Dow Jones had lost more than 40 percent of its value. Gone were the savings of tens of thousands of investors. Gone also was a prosperous future. Investors, brokers, and bankers were all big losers. Investors lost personal savings and had no way of paying off debts, due to the fact they had bought most of their stocks on margin. Brokers wound up with fewer clients and most went out of business because no one was left to satisfy bankers. It was those same bankers, of course, who had lent anywhere from 50 percent to 90 percent of their deposits to investors to buy stocks—you guessed it—on margin. But because there was little cash to go around, millions of dollars in bank loans went unpaid.

Without a doubt, margin was one of the key reasons for the Crash of 1929. And that crash was the primary trigger for the Great Depression.

Depression: 1930 –1937

Following the crash, most Americans were in shock over the magnitude of money that had disappeared. Comedians had no choice but to make fun of how much they lost trading stocks. Suddenly, the Roaring Twenties seemed like a majestic, make-believe land far, far away, that would never be inhabited again.

If any good were to come out of the crash, it would be the death of the foolishness and individualism the Roaring Twenties had given birth to. America was about to see what it was really made of. The world would soon find out whether the nation would run and hide from its problems or work hard despite them, knowing better days would eventually return.

Unfortunately, the attitude of run and hide lingered for the first two or three years of the depression. Times had to get worse before they could get better. Most Americans had no place to turn. The government had not planned for a depression and had no way of stopping it once it started. There were no government programs, such as unemployment insurance or welfare, for the needy to fall back on.

But as bad as things were, leaders tried to comfort the nation with the thought that the crisis would be short-lived. And there were signs early on that they might be right. By the spring of 1930, the Dow Jones had rebounded from a low of 198.69 on Nov. 13, 1929, to a high of 293.43 on April 12—a 48 percent jump. President Hoover seized on this trend as an indication that the worst was over. "We have now passed the worst and with continued unity of effort shall rapidly recover,"[11] Hoover told the country.

However, the bounce turned out to be nothing more than a bear market rally. Investors who thought they could win back losses became losers once again in another price free-fall during the summer and autumn. This final collapse was the last straw for the struggling economy, as production decreased each and every month that year.

American's middle class, after having flourished during the 1920s, was on the brink of vanishing by 1931. Millions were left homeless, with no hope of regaining the prosperity they had enjoyed just a few years earlier. "The feeling of helplessness was a caul whose weight could bring the strongest man down in tears, as a boy discovered when he came upon his father in the empty coal bin of the family's house in Brookline, Massachusetts. The father was crying."[12] "We had owned a small bakery that had failed a few months before," the boy remembered. "Things would get worse for us later on, and for a couple years we were in really bad shape, but to me the low point of the depression will always be the sight of my father that day, crying in the coal bin."[13]

Similar stories abounded, as dreams turned into real-life nightmares. In New York City, during the "night, some 3,300 street people, including as many as 100 women, found sleep on the beds, benches and floors of the six-story Municipal Lodging House on East Twenty-fifth Street. Thousands more clustered wherever they could in what would come to be called 'Hoovervilles,' in bitter mockery of the president, shantytowns constructed of everything that came to hand, from packing crates to hundreds of tin cans flattened out and nailed to boards. This was just the beginning of a long period of great suffering for many Americans."[14]

"Drifters," who literally did not own anything but the clothes on their back, crisscrossed America in search of work. Farmers were especially hard hit. Many lost farms to bankers, or to buyers who bought them out for pennies on the dollar. Prices for their products had fallen so much that they couldn't make a profit selling their crops.

A 1932 event in Chicago came to define just how far American had fallen. In the book *Since Yesterday*, author Frederick Lewis Allen writes about an American woman who said, "One vivid, gruesome moment of those dark days we shall never forget. We saw a crowd of some 50 men fighting over a barrel of garbage, which had been set outside the back door of a restaurant. American citizens fighting for scraps of food like animals."[15]

In that same year, on July 8, the Dow Jones index hit a bottom of 41.22, an eighty-nine percent drop from the high in September 1929. But it would take more than five years under Franklin D. Roosevelt for America to pull itself up by the bootstraps. Of course, by the time America did put itself back on a path to a more prosperous future, yet another crisis was around the corner. And President Roosevelt would a short time later address a joint session of Congress and announce that, "yesterday, Dec. 7, 1941—a date which will live in infamy— the United States was suddenly and deliberately attacked." And World War II would deliver still more hard times for the nation.

The Next Great Depression

People in general, and especially Americans, tend to have very short memories. Besides having poor memories, we tend to be arrogant. It is in large part because of those two characteristics that America is headed for another great depression.

Our current leaders, who keep telling us everything looks rosy, are actually leading us down a road of no return. And even as the economy goes from struggling to recession, our leaders, in their arrogance, will blame everything and everyone else but themselves. President Bush will have a difficult time admitting he is at fault. He will blame the Federal Reserve. He will blame Alan Greenspan. He may even blame former President Clinton. Bush will never take personal responsibility for creating the real estate bubble that is about to burst. My hope, though, is that he will prove me wrong and at some point level with the nation.

In the Wrong Place at the Wrong Time

The irreversible damage to the economy began when President Bush and the Federal Reserve artificially halted a normal business cycle and left us with a mini-recession in the early part of 2001. Bush prides himself for stopping a possible major recession in its tracks. He and the Fed did that by slashing interest rates to their lowest level in 40 years. The low rates provided cheap money for a huge number of Americans. However, a quote from Al Friedberg of Welling@Weeden.com on March 23, 2001, states that the extraordinarily low interest rates were not what America needed and in fact may lead to other problems. "Resources have been mis-allocated because of the cheapness of the credit in both stock and credit markets," Friedberg stated, "so, you're not going to solve the problem by making money cheaper again."[16] Furthermore, whatever economic expansion we've had over the last two years has come from more and more debt, not savings. Another way to look at this is the comparison to baseball's illegal use of steroids. All those that used the illegal drug are fakes. The current economy is the same. It's not real. The inevitable correction to this credit bubble will be very painful, and will trigger a depression of historic proportions. It's too bad we didn't learn from history and forgot the insight Gotfried Haberler provided for us in 1937. In his book *Prosperity and Depression*, Haberler writes: "The length and severity of depressions depend partly on the magnitude of the 'real' maladjustments which developed during the preceding boom, and partly on the aggravating monetary and credit conditions."[17]

As of July 2005, President Bush had his work cut out for him. The last thing Bush wants, of course, is for the artificially inflated stock market bubble, housing bubble, and credit bubble to start bursting on his watch. But, unfortunately, Bush will not be able to keep at bay forever the painful and inevitable corrections to the imbalances that have been caused by his easy money policy. Give the president credit; he has done a great job keeping the general population confident in the system. However, the damage has already been done and there is no turning back.

To save his own party, the Bush administration should have let Senator John Kerry of Massachusetts win the November 2004 election. But, of course, Kerry lost a close battle. And consequently Kerry will not be asked to shoulder any blame for the fall when it occurs. Instead, just like Hoover and the Republican Party in the days of the Great Depression, Bush and his modern-day GOP gang are going to have all the blame laid at their feet. As a result, don't expect another Republican president for the next 20 years.

Indeed, when it's all said and done, Bush could wind up being remembered as the worst president in U.S. history. His approval rating at the start of his second term was the lowest since that of the late President Richard Nixon, who was forced to resign in his second term because of the Watergate scandal. Don't be surprised if Bush suffers a similar fate. The president won't go down easily, but if the depression starts around the middle of Bush's second term, look for many to demand his impeachment.

His most disgraceful legacy, however, will be the towns that will bear his name. Look for hundreds of cities to fill with the ranks of unemployed people, and for those frustrated Americans to dub their communities "Bushtowns" as they point their fingers in Washington's direction. Bush may very well take his place in history next to Hoover, as another president who was in the wrong place at the wrong time.

The Abyss

The next year or two will be critical for the stock market and economy. If the writers of *The Fourth Turning* are correct—and I believe they are—2005–2008 will be the beginning of crisis and up to 20 years of turmoil and despair. Millions of Americans have never experienced anything like what is coming. In the 48 years I have lived, I vaguely remember the 1975 fuel shortage, the 1987 stock market crash, and the early 1990s coastal real estate collapse. But most of those alive today have never seen a bear market like the one that devoured investors in 1929. If today's investors thought the first leg down in today's bear market was bad, the next leg will crush them. We will not know what hit us. We will have no clue what happened. Maybe our first thought will be, "Isn't this to happen to our children or our children's children? Why now? Why me?"

American's psychology, which we discussed in Chapter 2, will determine the precise start of the depression. In the book *The Fourth Turning*, authors Strauss and Howe actually predicted that one of the catalysts to start the Crisis could be a global terrorist group blowing up an aircraft. And certainly, 9/11 was a wake-up call. However, nothing really changed. Culture wars still rage. America remains divided. Therefore, our nation's spend-until-you-drop philosophy and the-one-with-the-most-toys-wins mentality are not going to change without another, very severe, wake-up call.

Meanwhile, during the first part of 2005, government officials and economists focused so heavily on inflation that they have set themselves up to be blind-sided by the downward spiral of deflation. As we have seen so far in the 2005, the Dow Jones has struggled to stay above 10,000, which many believe to be a critical psychological level for the markets. Once the Dow Jones matches its October 20, 2002, low of 7181, we will have reached the point of no return. The amount of money that will be lost in the next leg down will be nothing short of staggering. Trillions of dollars will vanish. When the Dow Jones index falls below the point of no return, the re-inflated stock market and the housing bubble will burst and the worst depression in history will be only months away. As 2006 approaches, consumers will be forced to cut back on spending. Deflation will begin to rear its ugly head as debt-conscious consumers focus on paying bills and shop for better deals. Price wars and competition will heat up. Companies will do whatever they can to maintain their market shares. All this will cause the economy to contract and force businesses to lay people off.

Most industries will be affected, but none worse than housing and construction. Since 1998, homebuilders, believing the robust economy would crank forever, have built millions of new houses nationwide. In fact, the U.S. Commerce Department reported in February 2005 that the nation saw a record $998 billion pumped into construction in 2004. New-home construction was up a stunning 14 percent from the year before. A record $543 billion was spent on building houses alone. But by 2008, many of these homes will be empty, as over-capacity becomes the standard for more than a decade.

Don't Believe Them

In order to save the Republican Party, Bush will have no choice but to continue to insist that the economy is purring along just fine when, in fact, it is on the verge of collapse. Government officials will make the same mistake as the Hoover administration did in 1930. As Hoover claimed the economy of the early 1930s was improving, the Bush administration will maintain that everything is under control. But eventually, his administration will be forced by the public and media to admit that the economy is spinning out of control. By 2008—if not sooner—it will be clear that America is mired in a severe depression.

Even so, the government will do its best to convince the public that the economy is about to turn a corner. And because of this deception, a majority of Americans won't believe the existence of a depression until they are actually standing in line with their neighbors, waiting to withdraw their hard-earned savings. Unfortunately, only the first ones in line will receive any money. "Bank runs" a la 1930 will occur in every state. Thousands of banks will close their doors and claim bankruptcy.

Two Scenarios, Possibly Three

As we have been saying, a depression is imminent. It is not a question of if, but when. As far as severity, there are three potential scenarios: The first is a depression milder than the 1930s variety. The second is a massive depression that leads to a total collapse of the economy and destroys the middle class, leaving only the very rich and very poor. This latter scenario could prove so destructive that it could trigger the dividing up of the United States into several different countries, like the old Soviet Union that was carved up after the fall of communism.

The third scenario falls somewhere in the middle between the two extremes. In that case, we would look for a depression worse than the Great Depression, but marked by recovery several years later. Obviously, the first scenario would be the least damaging.

As for timing, the depression is likely to start during President Bush's current term, and the pace and severity could determine whether he remains in office through 2008. One thing is certain: the contraction will linger until all the imbalances created by all the bubbles are corrected. This will take several years, and perhaps as many as twenty years.

The approaching winter will unleash an unrelenting toll on American's middle class. At no time in history has the middle class been so prosperous, and yet so vulnerable. In order for most middle-class families to sustain their standard of living, both parents must work. If just one of them loses his or her job, those parents' ability to pay their bills and provide for their families becomes extremely difficult. And, so, with the coming depression, families with a mortgage, credit card debt, and car loans will be forced to cut back drastically or risk losing everything they worked for. Many will find themselves living with relatives or, worse, homeless. Millions will find it impossible even to provide for bare necessities.

Some will have to beg for food and clothes. Children will have trouble staying in school—not because of bad grades but because their parents won't have the money to pay for their education and clothing. Teens will have no choice but to mature quickly and take on more responsibility to help their families survive. Americans will truly feel that they have fallen into the abyss, a bottomless chasm impossible to climb out of.

The majority of Americans have seen only good times or mildly difficult times. We have been given whatever our hearts desired. We have done everything under the sun. America has enjoyed the world's highest standard of living for more than 60 years. Because of our prosperity, the vast majority of us won't even entertain the thought that America is destined for a horrific fall from grace. But people said similar things about the "unsinkable" *Titanic*. The approaching winter will be a long, cold, and bitter one. For millions of Americans, it will deliver the worst conditions they have ever lived through. And those conditions will trigger a shift from trying to collect the most toys to trying to survive. Just making it one more day will become a monumental task.

Chapter 5

Recovery?

Once the majority of Americans finally realize—and accept—the reality that America has slipped into a depression, the recovery will begin. It will not be pleasant. Personal sacrifice, teamwork, and patience for what will seem like an eternity will be required for this return to normalcy. Americans will have to first forgive the very people that helped start this approaching depression: government leaders such as President Bush, for bankrupting America, and Federal Reserve Chairman Alan Greenspan, for encouraging the largest credit bubble in history to be formed. Americans also will have to forgive themselves for living beyond their means, blindly believing government leaders and failing to plan and save in a prudent manner for the future.

Who Will Lead Us?

As we said before, if America is going to recover from this mother of all depressions reasonably quickly, we are going to have to find a leader with the character of an Abraham Lincoln, the president who led the United States to victory in the Civil War and helped to abolish slavery. We will need a leader like Franklin D. Roosevelt, whose great determination and vision led the nation back up from the Great Depression. America will need a leader who is neither extreme right nor extreme left. The depth of the unprecedented crisis will require a leader who is more concerned about helping the poor and homeless than winning a second term.

As well, we will need a leader who will not lie, if that, of course, is even possible. We will need a leader with the courage to challenge the rich to do their part, to contribute to charity the same percentage they gave during the boom years. America will need a leader who has a genuine humility, someone who doesn't just say "God bless America" because it sounds good, but because they truly rely on the Creator rather than himself or herself. And, America, it may be time that we select a woman to lead us in 2008.

For the sake of our international security, we will need someone who can address head on and fix the very serious problems Bush has created abroad. It is obvious that the number of countries with a dislike for the United States has multiplied since he took office. President Bush's quest for a worldwide democracy may indeed be commendable. The freedoms we have enjoyed for nearly 230 years are the envy of the world. And most of us would love to see a world without dictators. But at the same time, many have the conviction that "bullying" world leaders into running their governments the way the United States does is flat-out wrong. These

Americans would more than likely agree with an old quote from cowboy comedian Will Rogers, who said, "If there is one thing that we do worse than any other nation, it is try and manage somebody else's affairs."

Furthermore, some Americans realize that the example we have set in running up record government and consumer debt is all that many world leaders need to say no to democracy. It is a shame that our leaders have made the United States the largest debtor country in the world. And all that talk about freedom? What freedom do we really have, when we owe so much debt? America, we need perhaps most of all a leader who will humble out and admit that those who have directed our affairs these last 4½ years have been arrogant, prideful, and more concerned about pursuing their own interests than those of the country as a whole. And that leader will have to humbly go to our creditors—foreign nations—and ask them to forgive our debt.

Meanwhile, let us pray that one of the bold declarations in President Bush's second inaugural address doesn't come back to haunt us, just as a statement by former President Hoover did some 75 years ago. Bush, you'll remember, declared, "It is the policy of the United States to seek and support the growth of democratic movements and institutions in every nation and culture, with the ultimate goal of ending tyranny." Hoover had a different goal, but one that was every bit as lofty and sweeping in scope. "We have not yet reached the goal," Hoover said. "But we shall soon, with the help of God, be in sight of the day when poverty shall be banished from this nation." We all know what happened to Hoover's goal; instead of ushering in an era where only prosperous people walked the streets of America, it gave way to the Great Depression—and record poverty levels. We can only shudder at the thought of where Bush's goal may actually lead.

We Are Our Brother's Keeper

By the end of the economic winter, more than 30 percent of Americans will have lost their jobs. Many of them will be homeless and have no choice but to beg for basic necessities, things we all take for granted today. Because the majority of us—the herd—will err on the pessimistic side during these years, Americans will sense the need to be protective and cautious. The rich and those who keep their jobs will be tempted to be uncaring and look down on those with nothing but the shirts on their backs. Yet it will be incumbent on the rich to help rescue the country by uniting to feed, clothe, and shelter the poor. Large cities throughout the country are going to have to organize and supply numerous soup kitchens in order to feed the masses that will have become poor overnight.

We must avoid, at all cost, a situation like that which occurred in the Great Depression, where millions of acres of crops were destroyed because of the deflated prices. Farmers, in order to save money and avoid greater losses, decided to plow under their crops. As well, livestock in the millions were destroyed as part of a last-ditch strategy to halt the free-fall of prices that had been brought about by overproduction. All this led to one of the most shocking ironies of the Great Depression: Millions went without food and clothing even as surplus supplies of those commodities were destroyed—the very supplies that could have done so much good.

During this rapidly approaching next depression, those of us who can do something to help must do so. Americans must unify and help those who will be beaten down by the kind of severe trials most of us are unfamiliar with. If the rich, and those who manage to keep their jobs, want to sustain their way of life, they will have to pool their resources and help save America. In 1930, it was often heard on the streets of America: "Brother, can you spare me a dime?" Look for something similar to be spoken as this first major depression of the new millennium takes hold—with an adjustment, of course, to reflect today's values. Don't be surprised if you hear someone say, "Brother, can you spare me a dollar?" And we must not turn a deaf ear. We all must give our fellow Americans something to hope for.

America, We Have Recovered Before

After every crisis, dating back to the day we won our independence, we have always found a way to snap back. In 1781, after we sent the Brits back where they came from, defeated and shamed, we were free. Free from British law. Free from British taxes. It was a time our forefathers never forgot because it was the glorious birth of a great nation.

In 1860, the United States did not want war, but it happened anyway. The Civil War was the bloodiest ever to occur on American soil. More than 600,000 Americans died. During this horrific crisis, America was on the verge of destroying itself. And the recovery from that crisis was excruciatingly slow and painful. Still, it happened. America found a way to bounce back with resilience.

And, of course, there was 1930, the advent of the worst depression in history until now. After America depleted its excesses and overcapacities, which corrected the imbalances, the country was on its way back up. Then came World War II and more hard times, which postponed the long-anticipated recovery for even longer. But after the war, Americans would enjoy prosperity like never before. American recovered once again and became one of the most popular countries in the world. Everyone wanted to come here to live.

But will America survive this time? Perhaps every American will ask that question at some point during the next several years. As those hardy

Americans of the Great Depression fell on their knees in the 1930s and '40s, we will once again fall to our knees and ask God for deliverance.

Conclusion

This book was written to wake Americans up to the very real possibility, and in fact strong likelihood, that we will live through a monumental crisis like the kind that historically visits us every 75 years. The facts that an approaching economic winter is upon us are very clear.

You may agree that a depression is coming, or you may disagree. If you disagree, then you may want to ask yourself some questions. The first might be, "Who is going to pay all our debt?" Another might be, "How do I think we will avoid going through a cycle that occurs in America every 75 or 80 years?"

And ask yourself this: "Why do most people believe that the 1990s and the early 2000s were a repeat of the Roaring Twenties, but yet virtually no one expects the 1930s to repeat after our roaring period?" Last, but not least, ask, "When the same kind of speculation is occurring in the housing market that occurred in the stock market, what makes me so sure it won't implode just as the NASDAQ did between 2000 and 2002?

I know I've painted a bleak picture of the future, one that is not easy to accept. It wasn't easy for me to accept, either. Before 9/11, I did not believe a depression would, or even could, happen in my lifetime. For me, it was always a problem my grandchildren would have to grapple with one day many years from now. But when I considered the evidence and the idea that an actual full-blown depression could happen, I became frightened and concerned. Then I read *The Fourth Turning* a second time. It convinced me that a depression not only could happen but that an economic crisis of historic proportions was indeed imminent. And I was determined to do something about it. Thus was born *The Approaching Winter: The Next Great Depression.*

In closing, this book was written not for the scholar, but for Americans like myself. It is straight to the point and delivered with conviction. I sincerely hope that I am wrong. But, if I am right, may God be with us and have mercy on us.

Endnotes

Chapter 1

1   Myron E. Forbes, President, Pierce Arrow Motor Car Co., January 12, 1928
    www.cyberhaven.com

2   Calvin Coolidge, Dec. 4, 1928
    www.gold-eagle.com

3   Paul Block, editorial, 1929
    www.gold-eagle.com

4   Irving Fisher, Professor of Economics, Yale University, 1929
    www.quotesforall.com

5   Gold and Economic Freedom, Alan Greenspan,
    The Objectivist, July, 1966

6   Kevin Rayburn, a time line of the 1920s

7   President Theodore Roosevelt, (1858-1919),
    www.brainyquote.com

8   William Strauss and Neil Howe, *The Fourth Turning*, Broadway, 1997

9   ibid

10 ibid

11 Copyright by the New York Times Agency. Reprinted with permission

12 Steve Hochberg and Pete Kendall, *The Elliott Wave Financial Forecast*, a publication of Prechter's Elliot Wave International, July 2005

Chapter 2

1 Charles Mackay, *Extraordinary Popular Delusions and the Madness in Crowds*, Barnes & Noble Inc., June, 1994

2 Robert R. Prechter, Jr. *The Wave Principle of Human Social Behavior and The New Science of Socionomics*, New Classics Library, 1999

Chapter 3

1 Bureau of the Public Debt:
www.publicdebt.treas.gov/opd/opdpenny.htm

2 Grandfather Federal Government Debt Report:
http//mwhodges.home.att.net/debt.htm

3 ibid

4 Martin Crutsinger, The Associated Press, ABC News: "Budget Deficit Surges to $113.9 Billion in February," March 10, 2005; Department of the Treasury; CBO. www.cbo.gov

5 Frederick W. Stakelbeck, Jr., "The Role of Credit Cards in an Increasingly Indebted World Economy," www.phil.frb.org

6 Paul Muolo, executive editor, National Mortgage News, "2004 and 2003: The Years In Review,"
www.naitonalmortgagenews.com

7 "Bush signs tougher bankruptcy bill into law," MSNBC.com, The Associated Press

8 William Branigin, *Washington Post*, "U.S. Consumer Debt Grows at Alarming Rate," January 12, 2004

9   Alan Greenspan, before the Economic Club of New York, New York, March 2, 2004, www.federalreserve.gov

10 Alan Greenspan, before a credit union conference, February 22, 2004, www.rgi.com

11 Alan Greenspan, before the America's Community Bankers, October 26, 2004, www.forbes.com

12 Bridgewater Associates, Westport, Connecticut, March 2004 Report

13 Tome Kelly, STLtoday.com, "Second-home purchases surprise real estate economists," April 13, 2005, www/stltoday.com

14 Kevin Duffy, Prudent Bear.com, "Honey, I shrunk the Net Worth," March 7, 2005

15. California Association of Realtors, July 25, 2005, www.car.org

16. U.S. Census Bureau, Census of Housing, Historical Census of Housing Tables, Home Values, *Adjusted for inflation, 2000 dollars www.census.gov/hhes/www/housing/census/historic/values.html

17. www.realtor.org, Walter Molony, "Existing Home-Sales Smash Record Again," July 25, 2005

18 American Dream Downpayment Act of 2003, December 16, 2003, www.consumer-guides.info/housing/Home_Owership/

19 Fred E. Foldvary, "Real Estate and Business Cycles: Henry George's Theory of the Trade Cycle"

20 Robert R Prechter Jr., Conquer the Crash, John Wiley and Sons, Ltd. 2002, Reproduced with permission

21 Bryan B Sterling and Frances N. Sterling, *Reflection and Observations*, Crown, 1982

22 Alan Greenspan, before the Senate Banking Committee, April 20, 2004

23 Alan Greenspan, before the Joint Economic Committee, May 21, 2003

Chapter 4

1 Maury Klein, *Rainbow's End: The Crash of 1929*, Oxford University Press, 2001, p 142

2 Herbert Hoover, speech accepting the Republican nomination, Palo Alto, California.
http://historymatters.gmu.edu/d/5063.html

3 Maury Klein, *Rainbow's End: The Crash of 1929*, Oxford University Press, 2001, p 158

4 H. B. Watkins, *The Hungry Years*, Henry Holt and Company, LLC, 1999, p 10

5 Maury Klein, *Rainbow's End: The Crash of 1929*, Oxford University Press, 2001, p 12

6 Robert S. McElvaine, *The Great Depression*, Three Rivers Press, 1993, p 17

7 Karen Blumenthal, *Six Days In October: The Stock Market Crash of 1929*, Atheneum, 2002, p 13

8 ibid, p 19

9 ibid, pp 61, 62

10 Barbara Silberdick Feinberg, *Black Tuesday:The Stock Market Crash of 1929*, Millbrook Press, 1995, pp 7, 8

11 President Hoover, March 1930

12 H. B. Watkins, *The Hungry Years*, Henry Holt and Company, LLC, 1999, p 55

13 Charles A. Jellison, *Tomatoes Were Cheaper: Tales from the Thirties*, Syracuse University Press, Syracuse, NY. 1977

14 H. B. Watkins, *The Hungry Years*, Henry Holt and Company, LLC, 1999, p 61

15 Frederick Lewis Allen, *Since Yesterday*, Perennial-Harpercollins, July 1986

16 Welling@Weeden.com, Al Freidberg, March 23, 2001

17 Gotfried Von Haberier, *Prosperity and Depression*, University Press of the Pacific, 2001

Books for Additional Reading

The Fourth Turning, William Strauss and Neil Howe, Broadway, 1997

The Wave Principle of Human Social Behavior and the New Science of Socionomics, Robert R. Prechter, Jr., New Classics Library, 1999

The Hungry Years, T.H. Watkins, Henry Holt and Company, LLC, 1999

Rainbow's End The Crash of 1929, Maury Klein, Oxford University Press, 2001

Six Days in October: The Stock Market Crash of 1929, Karen Blumenthal, Atheneum, 2002

Black Tuesday: The Stock Market Crash of 1929, Barbara Silberdick Feinberg, Millbrook Press, 1995

The Great Depression, Robert S. McElvaine, Three Rivers Press, 1993

Conquer The Crash, Robert R. Prechter, Jr., John Wiley & Sons Ltd., 2002

Running on Empty, Peter G. Peterson, Farrar, Straus and Giroux, 2004

www.ingramcontent.com/pod-product-compliance
Lightning Source LLC
Chambersburg PA
CBHW022110170526
45157CB00004B/1574